PR☼MISES

CONFIDENCE FOR TODAY.
A GUARANTEE FOR TOMORROW.

TABLE OF
CONTENTS

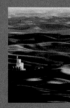

Here's
the Plan

1. Grow closer to God as you understand and study His Word.

2. Study the intro weeks individually. Study weeks 1-6 with a group.

3. Know and receive the promises of God.

You may notice the theme of a moving sun throughout this guide. The daily rising of the sun has been a constant reminder of the dependability and faithfulness of God to His promises.

PSALM 148:3-6

3 Praise him, sun and moon;
  praise him, all you shining stars.
4 Praise him, you highest heavens
  and you waters above the skies.

5 Let them praise the name of the Lord,
  for at his command they were created,
6 and he established them for ever and ever—
  he issued a decree that will never pass away.

How This
Guide Works

READ THE CHAPTER
- Concept
- Context
- Passage
- What Does This Mean for Us?
- What Do I Do with This?

INTERACT WITH THE CONCEPTS
- Take notes in the margins.
- Write out answers to the questions.
- Memorize the weekly verse.
  (cards located in the back of this guide)

TALK ABOUT IT WITH YOUR GROUP
Starting with Week One:
"WHAT ARE GOD'S PROMISES TO ME?"

INTRO
PART ONE

HOW DO I LEARN TO
TRUST GOD'S PROMISES?

NOTES

Concept

Wishes are uncertain. Dreams lack assurance. *But there is **power** in a promise.*

A promise is a wish or a dream backed by the confidence that only comes from a guarantee.

> *This is going to happen. You can count on it,*
> *because you can count on me.*

This guarantee draws its power from the reputation of the character of the one making the promise.

> *You know me. I have proven myself.*
> *You have seen me come through, time and time again.*

THERE IS POWER IN A PROMISE.

And a promise really only becomes valuable when you know what it is.

> *I have a plan for your life.*
> *I will bless your family.*
> *I will never leave you or forsake you.*
> *I have given you everything you need*
> *for the life you were created to live.*

We would appreciate these promises from anyone. But what if the God who created the heavens and Earth promised us each of these things?

NOTES

The challenge of a promise is the uncertainty. **What if I get my hopes up only to be disappointed?** A promise makes us vulnerable.

What if I get hurt?

The renowned French general Napoleon Bonaparte understood this. He said, **"The best way to keep one's word is not to give it."**

A promise is risky. It puts both the one who gives it and the one who receives it in danger of deep disappointment. God understands all of these things.

And yet, what if He was so bold that He swore these promises on the honor of His own name? What if these were only a few of the many promises God made to His people? What if we could learn to trust and experience these promises in our daily lives?

The incredible truth is, this is exactly what He's done. And so much more.

What does God give us to trust His promises? His Word. And there is no better guarantee of God's Word than the Living Word, the Word made flesh, Jesus Himself. A study into the promises of God is a study into the person of Jesus.

THE CHALLENGE OF A PROMISE IS THE UNCERTAINTY.
WHAT IF I GET MY HOPES UP ONLY TO BE DISAPPOINTED?
A PROMISE MAKES US VULNERABLE. WHAT IF I GET HURT?

NOTES

Context

One of Jesus' closest friends and followers was a man named Peter. Near the end of his life, Peter is leading a group of people who are facing incredible adversity. They are afraid for their lives—with good reason. And yet Peter reminds them Jesus has given them everything they could ever need through His divine power.

Why would Peter feel this way?
How could he be so confident?

Peter knew what many of us do not know. **Peter understood the significance of God's promises because he understood God's promises are founded on another Bible word: "covenant."**

"Covenant" is a word of deep biblical significance. In fact, covenant is a theme that runs through the entirety of Scripture.

A covenant is a relational agreement; it's a partnership toward a specific purpose, treated with the utmost commitment and respect.

In the Hebrew language, you do more than make a covenant—you cut one. The phrase in English "make a covenant" most often comes from the Hebrew *karat berit*, which translates to "cut a covenant."

In our world, an agreement becomes official when you sign it. In the ancient world, they would cut/sacrifice an animal not to be cruel but to demonstrate the significance of the commitment. It cost you something valuable.

This is where language like "cut a deal," or "strike a bargain," comes from. It is a life-and-death level bond made with the assurance only possible when you put the reputation of your character and name on the line.

In the Bible, covenants were made between God and man, between two people, between two kings, between two families, and between two nations. These relational agreements were more than a contract—they were partnerships intended to build together toward a common goal.

Covenants were often accompanied by oaths, ceremonies, sacrifices, and the exchange of gifts to signify importance.

Once you understand this, you will consistently see this "covenantal language" as a thread throughout God's Word communicating a depth of significance you could easily miss.

NOTES

COV·E·NANT
noun

a relational agreement; a partnership toward a specific purpose, treated with the utmost commitment and respect.

NOTES

Passage

2 PETER 1:2-4

2 Grace and peace be yours in abundance through the knowledge of God and of Jesus our Lord. 3 His divine power has given us everything we need for a godly life through our knowledge of him who called us by his own glory and goodness. 4 Through these he has given us his very great and precious promises, so that through them you may participate in the divine nature, having escaped the corruption in the world caused by evil desires.

GET MORE OUT OF YOUR READING

Does something stick out to you? Do you have questions about a passage? It is helpful to underline ideas or phrases that stand out to you or write down a question to ask later in your group.

What Does This Mean for Us?

NOTES

Is there anyone who does not want grace and peace?

"Grace and peace" was a common greeting in the ancient world because everyone wanted them. We still want them—*need them*—today.

Grace is a gift we cannot earn. Peace does not mean we have no problems. Peace is God's presence giving us the sense that things in our world are right.

Peter is saying that grace and peace are promises that come from Jesus. More than a wise moral teacher, friend, or founder of a religion, Jesus has divine power—power that comes from God—because He is God.

He's given us everything we need for a godly life by His own glory and goodness. Again, this is covenantal language. Jesus is entering into a partnership with us—a significant commitment—and He's so invested He's guaranteeing our success.

But Peter does not stop there. Now remember, Peter and the people he's writing to are in life-and-death danger. Yet Peter tells us that Jesus gives us everything we need, and through these promises we get to participate (covenant language again) in the divine nature. This may not sound like a big deal, but it is.

The divine nature is the person and power of God at work in us. We are not prisoners of the evil desire and corruption of the world. But we don't escape through gritting our teeth and trying harder.

We change as we trust and receive the promises of God.

We are designed for covenant. Life itself and the greatest personal accomplishments feel empty without it because we serve a covenant God who made us in His image.

His goal is higher than getting us out of our problems into a good life. He wants to change us to be more like Him.

Being in a covenant with God shows us what God is like. He always comes through on His purpose. God always goes above and beyond in His partnerships.

NOTES

WE ARE DESIGNED FOR COVENANT.

What Do I Do with This?

What do you think about when you hear the word "God"?

Do you think: Faithful? Trustworthy? A loving Father who keeps His promises?

This is how He describes Himself. And this is how He wants to relate to you.

Are you disappointed with a promise you have not received?

Have you blamed this on God?

Are you sure He's not working on it right now—even though you can't see it?

SUMMARY

When God makes a promise to us, He's making a covenant. This is a partnership— a significant relational agreement given with deep commitment.

Know therefore that the Lord your God is God; he is the faithful God, keeping his covenant of love to a thousand generations of those who love him and keep his commandments.

Deuteronomy 7:9

INTRO
PART TWO

WHAT'S THE BIBLE'S BIG MESSAGE
ABOUT GOD'S PROMISES?

NOTES

Concept

You can read the entire Bible through the theme of covenant. In fact, the words "testament" and "covenant" are interchangeable; so whenever you read the Old Testament or the New Testament in your Bible, you are reading about the Old and New "Covenant." The idea of covenant is even woven into how we structure the Bible.

From the beginning to the end, this is how God's covenant works: God creates men and women in His image with the intended purpose of partnering with them to enjoy relationships and to join Him in His good work.

This is who God is. He has not changed.

Because this theme of covenant spans all of Scripture, there is some discussion among experts as to the number of major covenants in the Bible. The most common response is "five" because these correspond to the names of the people who partnered with God.

To trace the overlying message of God's promises, it greatly helps us to understand the larger covenant plans He lays out in His Word.

Based on this view, there are at least eight major covenants in the Bible:

NOTES

1. The Eden Covenant
Genesis 1:26-31

God makes mankind (male and female) in His image, to steward (manage) creation—the animals, the land, and the plants. He blesses them and tells them to be fruitful and multiply—to fill the earth and care for everything God has given them. He calls this covenant partnership "good."

He still has not broken this promise. He's still blessing anyone who joins Him in this partnership.

2. The Adam Covenant
Genesis 2:15-25; 3:8-24

God enters into a partnership with the first man Adam. God places Adam in the Garden and promises to bless Him. God immediately makes good on this promise by giving Eve to Adam because He said it is not good for people to be alone. God gives Adam one stipulation—do not eat from a certain tree—and before long, Adam and Eve break the deal.

Despite this, God does not give up on or abandon them, but He does modify their partnership: work becomes exceedingly difficult and lacks fulfillment, childbirth is characterized by pain, and relationships between men and women are greatly complicated.

NOTES

3. The Noah Covenant
Genesis 6:9-22; Genesis 9:1-17

The world is filled with evil and wickedness, but God finds a partner in a man named Noah. God promises to preserve Noah and his family if he builds an ark and loads it with rescued animals. Though it has never rained, the world is flooded, God saves Noah and his family, blesses them, and gives the rainbow as a sign he'll never flood the earth again.

4. The Abraham Covenant
Genesis 12:1-5

God comes to an established 75-year-old man named Abram and He tells him to leave his land to go to a place God would show him. God promises to make this man with no children into a great nation and to make his name great. God changes Abram's name to Abraham and promises all the people on Earth would be blessed through him.

It took 25 years from the day God made this promise to Abraham for him to receive it, but the whole world continues to be blessed through this promise even today.

5. The Moses Covenant
Exodus 3, 20, and 34

God meets, in a burning bush, an 80-year-old shepherd who grew up in a palace in Egypt. God's solution to 400 years of pain is to partner with Moses to rescue His people from Egypt. Once God makes good on His promise to deliver millions of people, He calls Moses up on a mountain to give them ten commandments on

NOTES

how to live. This covenant will show them how to be His people, including specific instructions for worship and the forgiveness of sins.

God gives His commandments to Moses on tablets of stone. But Moses breaks the tablets when he discovers the people have already broken God's commands before he even made it down the mountain! So, Moses goes back and gets a second set of tablets from God to give to the people.

Despite their unfaithfulness, God does not give up on His people. He always preserves a group of His people, because of His partnership with Abraham.

6. The David Covenant
2 Samuel 7:11b-16

One of the ways the people broke God's covenant with Moses was their desire to be like every other nation. They wanted a king. The first king, Saul, was the cultural perception of a man's man—handsome, athletic, strong, and prideful. He failed. The second king, David, was flawed, overly emotional, but deeply committed to God. Although he made big mistakes, he was a man after God's heart.

Because of this, God makes a covenant agreement with David to establish his throne forever. God's intention was to bring the one true king, the king God always had for His people (Jesus), through the line of David. This Messiah— the chosen, anointed one of God—would fulfill all the covenant promises of God.

NOTES

7. The Covenant of the Promised Land
Deuteronomy 29

Near the end of Deuteronomy, God reaffirms the covenant He originally made with Abraham for His people. He has not forgotten His promise to give the people land. In fact, the land would come to be called the "Promised Land," the place where He will be their God.

In later generations, the people disobeyed God's commands and were taken away from the Promised Land. In these moments, as they lived as captives in foreign lands, this covenant promise reminded them they were meant for something greater.

While this promise does speak to an actual place, it also points back to the Eden Covenant: God is good and He has made an eternal partnership to bless His people as they enjoy a relationship with Him and enter in to His work.

8. The New Covenant
Jeremiah 31:33-34; 1 Corinthians 11:23-26;
Hebrews 10:19-23

God amends and fulfills all of the previous covenants through a new covenant instituted and guaranteed through the greatest extension of His person—the second and faithful Adam, the living Word, the true Passover Lamb, the true descendant of Abraham, the ultimate King of David's line, the door to the Promised Land—Jesus.

Every promise of God is completed, fulfilled, guaranteed, and found in Him.

This is the Bible's consistent message about the

promises of God. They are much more than a series of individual promises, like a book of gift certificates or a random collection of fortune cookie sayings.

God's promises are grand, eternal, and cosmic in their scope. And yet, they are deeply personal for you today.

But here is what we have to understand about God's covenant promises: We never make the first move. God is always reaching out to us to partner and work with Him—not because He needs us, but because He loves us. This is who He is. Always faithful. Always generous. Always loving. Always good.

In every situation God always gives us everything we need to love and worship Him.

His promises are so much better than our needs. He promises to give us Himself.

NOTES

NOTES

Context

We first meet Abram (who would later be called the much more familiar Abraham) in Genesis 11 through the heritage of his father, Terah. The Bible appears to imply God offered the promise of the land of Canaan to him but he settled and stopped in the land of Haran. God comes to Abram and tells him He would make him a great nation, He would make his name great, and through him all the people on Earth would be blessed.

Abram responds to these incredible promises and goes to the land of Canaan. It's filled with people but God promises to give his descendants the land, so Abram makes an altar and worships.

As you might imagine, significant problems quickly emerge. There's a famine in the land, so they go to Egypt (another Bible pattern). God blesses Abram like He promised and so his nephew Lot separates and ends up needing to be rescued.

Abram has seen enough to believe God is definitely doing something, but he's wrestling with it. So God comes and helps to strengthen his confidence in what He promised.

NOTES

Passage

GENESIS 15:1-6

1 After this, the word of the Lord came to

   Abram in a vision:

  "Do not be afraid, Abram.

   I am your shield

   your very great reward."

2 But Abram said, "Sovereign Lord, what can you give me since I remain childless and the one who will inherit my estate is Eliezer of Damascus?"

3 And Abram said, "You have given me no children; so a servant in my household will be my heir."

4 Then the word of the Lord came to him: "This man will not be your heir, but a son who is your own flesh and blood will be your heir." 5 He took him outside and said, "Look up at the sky and count the stars—if indeed you can count them." Then he said to him, "So shall your offspring be."

6 Abram believed the Lord, and he credited it to him as righteousness.

What Does This Mean for Us?

NOTES

ROMANS 4:16-25

[16] Therefore, the promise comes by faith, so that it may be by grace and may be guaranteed to all Abraham's offspring—not only to those who are of the law but also to those who have the faith of Abraham. He is the father of us all. [17] As it is written: "I have made you a father of many nations." He is our father in the sight of God, in whom he believed—the God who gives life to the dead and calls into being things that were not.

[18] Against all hope, Abraham in hope believed and so became the father of many nations, just as it had continued on pg 37

Abram was 75 and he had no children. He was understandably skeptical and afraid. God knew this about him and so He came to Abram and told him not to be afraid.

God doesn't get mad at Abram for struggling. Instead, He takes him outside and gives him a practical reminder of His faithfulness.

Look at all those stars. This is what I can do. If I can fill the universe with stars and keep them in their place, how hard is it for me to take care of your family?

This changes Abram. He believes. He has a very real reminder of this personal and loving God who makes good on His promises. And the Lord treats Abram's willingness to believe Him as righteousness.

This is a big deal. "Righteousness" is a legal term meaning "right standing." It means God does not agree to a partnership with us because we are perfect but because we trust Him.

It means if we are afraid or uncertain, God is not surprised. He comes to help us.

God's covenant with Abraham is like the umbrella covenant of the Old Testament. It covers all of us. We know this because the New Testament repeatedly makes the point that everyone—no matter where they're from or what their family did or didn't do—who believes like Abraham is part of His family. For example, Galatians 3:7 (NLT) says, "The real children of Abraham, then, are those who put their faith in God."

This means everything God promised Abraham, He also promises them.

This raises some important questions.

- How do we receive the promises of God?
- Do we earn them?
- Do we meet all of God's perfect standards?

If Abraham couldn't do that, we shouldn't be surprised that we can't either. But that's not how it works.

God's promises are not an inheritance distributed by a will. We don't have to be his natural descendants. The promise comes by faith—and the promise is guaranteed by God Himself. When we believe by faith these covenant promises apply to us, God generously includes us.

been said to him, "So shall your offspring be." [19] Without weakening in his faith, he faced the fact that his body was as good as dead—since he was about a hundred years old—and that Sarah's womb was also dead. [20] Yet he did not waver through unbelief regarding the promise of God, but was strengthened in his faith and gave glory to God, [21] being fully persuaded that God had power to do what he had promised. [22] This is why "it was credited to him as righteousness." [23] The words "it was credited to him" were written not for him alone, [24] but also for us, to whom God will credit righteousness—for us who believe in him who raised Jesus our Lord from the dead. [25] He was delivered over to death for our sins and was raised to life for our justification.

NOTES

What Do I Do with This?

Have you ever doubted one of God's promises?

Have you ever worried, *What if God doesn't come through?* Have you ever thought, *This is for special people...people who don't struggle like I do?*

You are not alone. This does not have to be the end.

God is not looking for a reason to get out of this deal. He wants to bless you. It may not look the way you imagined it, it may not happen on your timetable, but He's not holding out on you.

Remember, these promises come by faith. **Read Romans 4:16-25 out loud (pgs 36 and 37).** Memorize verse 16. When you feel distant from God's promises, remind yourself what God has promised you in His Word.

SUMMARY

God keeps His promises—this is one of the great themes of Scripture. And we are included in these covenant promises when we believe.

Therefore, the promise comes by faith, so that it may be by grace and may be guaranteed to all Abraham's offspring—not only to those who are of the law but also to those who have the faith of Abraham. He is the father of us all.

Romans 4:16

WEEK
ONE

WHAT ARE GOD'S
PROMISES TO ME?

NOTES

Concept

Discovering and tracing the theme of covenant throughout the Bible may be interesting. But in order for it to be meaningful, we have to understand how it applies to us.

How does it change our lives?
How does it impact today?

What are these promises God has made? Which of them were only for the person in the story? Which can we expect to receive ourselves? If only there were someone who could make it clear to us.

Even when we know what they are, we often have a hard time believing the incredible promises God has made to us.

Deep down we know we don't deserve them—especially when we blow it. We know all too well our inability to live up to our word. If we can't keep our promises, why would God keep His promises to us?

Once again, this is where Jesus comes to the rescue. He makes these promises real to us. He reminds us He has always upheld His end of the covenant with God. He lived a life of perfect obedience.

NOTES

2 PETER 1:3

His divine power has given us everything we need for a godly life through our knowledge of him who called us by his own glory and goodness.

2 CORINTHIANS 1:20a

For no matter how many promises God has made, they are "Yes" in Christ.

He did what we should have but could not. He avoided the temptations our self-control would not have been strong enough to overcome. As Peter told us, He gives us every one of His great promises—everything we need for a godly life.

As we will learn from another grateful recipient of the promises of God (a very important leader in the early church named Paul), God's promises are not yes and no. They are not maybe or maybe not.

All of God's promises are yes...in Jesus.

When we are in Him, and our hope is not in our ability to earn or work for these promises through our spiritual effort, we gain the confidence to know God is not holding out on us. He will come through on what He has promised.

NOTES

Context

What does Jesus do when He's finished working for His adopted earthly father, Joseph? How does He get ready to work for His heavenly Father preaching the gospel, healing the sick, and making disciples?

First, He's led by the Holy Spirit into the wilderness. The wilderness is where the people of God wandered for 40 years. The wilderness is a place where things are darkest and evil and demonic powers rule.

Second, Satan shows up and tempts Jesus, offering Him all kinds of earthly rewards. Jesus dismisses him based on the promises of God's Word.

Third, Jesus returns to His hometown in the power of the Spirit and goes to the synagogue with His family for their weekly worship service.

Think about what we've learned. Each of these actions is a response to a partnership God made with His people:

- The desire to join God in His mission is the Eden covenant.
- This first victory over Satan (with many more to come) is the Adam covenant.
- The faithfulness of God to lead Him through the wilderness is the Promised Land covenant.

And finally, in Luke 4:14-22 we find Jesus standing up and declaring that the prophetic passage in Isaiah was about Him. This was Jesus' first public declaration, telling everyone He had come to fulfill the New Covenant.

"'THE SPIRIT OF THE LORD IS ON ME, BECAUSE HE HAS ANOINTED ME TO PROCLAIM GOOD NEWS TO THE POOR. HE HAS SENT ME TO PROCLAIM FREEDOM FOR THE PRISONERS AND RECOVERY OF SIGHT FOR THE BLIND, TO SET THE OPPRESSED FREE, TO PROCLAIM THE YEAR OF THE LORD'S FAVOR.'" LUKE 4:18-19

NOTES

Passage

LUKE 4:14-22

14 Jesus returned to Galilee in the power of the Spirit, and news about him spread through the whole countryside. 15 He was teaching in their synagogues, and everyone praised him.

16 He went to Nazareth, where he had been brought up, and on the Sabbath day he went into the synagogue, as was his custom. He stood up to read, 17 and the scroll of the prophet Isaiah was handed to him. Unrolling it, he found the place where it is written:

18 "The Spirit of the Lord is on me, because he has anointed me to proclaim good news to the poor. He has sent me to proclaim freedom for the prisoners and

NOTES

recovery of sight for the blind, to set the oppressed free, 19 to proclaim the year of the Lord's favor."

20 Then he rolled up the scroll, gave it back to the attendant and sat down. The eyes of everyone in the synagogue were fastened on him. 21 He began by saying to them, "Today this scripture is fulfilled in your hearing."

22 All spoke well of him and were amazed at the gracious words that came from his lips. "Isn't this Joseph's son?" they asked.

What Does This Mean for Us?

NOTES

If you were in the synagogue in Nazareth that day, it would have sounded crazy to you too. Normal people do not stand up and say, "This promise from God, this section of the Bible spoken by the Spirit hundreds of years ago to Isaiah...it's about me."

This passage was well known by the people of God. It pointed to a day when God would send His promised Messiah to right every wrong in the world.

The year of the Lord's favor is more than the current date on the calendar—it's a new era, where the Spirit of God rescues people who are captive, helps people who are poor, gives sight to the blind, and restores the world to the way God always intended it to be.

When the people said, "Isn't this Joseph's son?", what they are saying is, "We know this guy. We watched him grow up. We know his family. There is no way this is who God was talking about!!"

Many people—maybe even most people—like Jesus and

His teaching. They see the value in the Golden Rule (do unto others...). They aspire to forgiving others so they will forgive them. They attempt to love their neighbors. These are admirable qualities they attempt to reach through their own spiritual discipline.

In this mode, Jesus is a wise teacher. He is a life coach. He is a spiritual consultant who offers advice you can take or leave.

We like this option, but it is not one Jesus Himself gives us.

Jesus cannot be a good teacher or a consultant because either He's lying to us (He knows this is not about Him), He's crazy (He does not know who He is, who God is, or who Isaiah is), or He is the ONLY WAY we can receive the promises of God.

Remember the important leader in the early church named Paul? He understood this very well. He violently opposed Jesus and His followers, until he met the resurrected Jesus in person. After this, Paul changed everything in his life (starting with his name) to tell everyone he could to put their trust in Jesus.

He wrote several letters to a group of people in a church who made lots of mistakes and did not keep their promises to God. He told them, because of Jesus and His faithfulness, we could trust that God would keep every promise.

He said that no matter how many promises God has made, they are all yes to us because of Jesus.

As we continue in this guide, we will discover these promises relate to the areas of our lives we care about the most.

NOTES

NO MATTER HOW MANY PROMISES GOD HAS MADE, THEY ARE ALL YES TO US BECAUSE OF JESUS.

NOTES

We do not approach the Bible like a Magic 8 Ball hoping what God promised to someone, somewhere He might do for us.

Instead, we read it knowing all of God's promises point to His Son, Jesus. And when we are in Him, we have the confidence—the guarantee—He will give us everything we need.

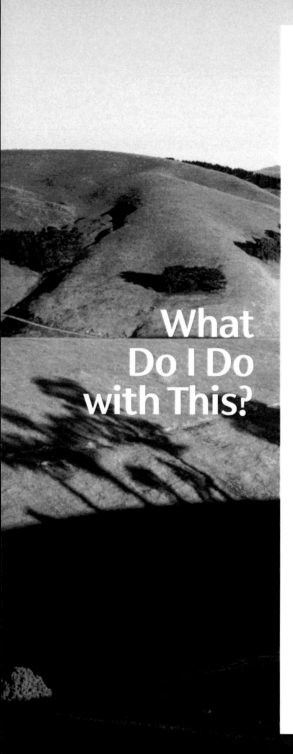

What Do I Do with This?

Do you ever struggle, wondering if God has forgotten about you? Do you ever feel unworthy of God's blessing?

Do you sometimes wonder whether the circumstances you are facing are the result of God's punishment?

Do you relate to Jesus as a wise teacher? A life coach? A spiritual guide?

This approach cannot produce the confidence or the guarantee God has for you. Remember, this is only possible when we put our trust in Jesus. He is the guarantee of all of God's promises. They come through Him.

Our confidence in the promises of God does not come from us.

We cannot earn His blessing.

Our poor choices often come with consequences, but they cannot separate us from God's blessing or our relationship with Jesus because we did not earn them in the first place.

SUMMARY

All of God's promises point us to Jesus. He is the ultimate expression of the love and goodness of God. And He is the way we receive everything God has for us.

For no matter how many promises God has made,
they are "Yes" in Christ.

2 Corinthians 1:20a

QUESTIONS

01   **Read 2 Corinthians 1:20a.** What do you think it means when the Bible says that all of God's promises are "Yes" in Christ?

02   What do you think it means to be "in Christ"?

03   Why do we sometimes have a hard time believing God's promises are for us?

04   Why does God keep His promises to us even when we fail?

05   Is there a time in your life when God showed you love and mercy, even when you had failed? What was the situation, and what did God do for you?

06   Have you fully surrendered your life to Christ and placed your trust in Him? Explain.

07   How is trusting in Jesus different than viewing Him as a wise teacher, a life coach, or a spiritual guide?

08   How has God transformed your life? Can you track some of the ways God has fulfilled His promises to you—even when you didn't deserve it?

WEEK TWO

HOW DO I STAND ON
GOD'S PROMISES?

NOTES

Concept

In order to stand you need a firm foundation—*terra firma* (the Latin phrase for dry land, solid ground). You need a well-built structure.

This makes you immovable. Secure. Confident. This is God's desire for us.

Hebrews 6:13 tells us, because He could find nothing greater to swear on, God swore His covenant promises to us using the reputation of His name as collateral. He did this so anyone who dared to believe Him would be greatly encouraged—and would have an anchor for their soul.

How can you tell when someone has learned to stand on God's promises? They have an anchor for their soul.

The Bible equates someone who constantly changes their mind with an infant who's blown around by the waves of different teachings given by cunning and crafty schemers.

In case you missed it, both of these are unstable on their own. Infants wobble, stumble, and consistently fall over as they learn to walk. If you've ever been at sea on a windy day, you know how hard it is to keep your feet with the deck shifting beneath you.

The only way we can stand with confidence on the promises of God is to know for certain where we stand with God.

HEBREWS 6:13
When God made his promise to Abraham, since there was no one greater for him to swear by, he swore by himself . . .

HEBREWS 6:18-19a
[18] God did this so that, by two unchangeable things in which it is impossible for God to lie, we who have fled to take hold of the hope set before us may be greatly encouraged.
[19] We have this hope as an anchor for the soul, firm and secure. . .

EPHESIANS 4:15
Instead, speaking the truth in love, we will grow to become in every respect the mature body of him who is the head, that is, Christ.

NOTES

Context

What is the most memorable night of your life? When you close your eyes, can you go back to that moment? Does it feel like you are right back in that place?

If we were to ask the disciples this same question, most of them would likely answer with the night Jesus was arrested, beaten, and sentenced to death.

The night did not start this way.

They had come to Jerusalem to celebrate the Passover, the holiest moment of the year—the moment they remembered God's faithfulness and the supernatural deliverance He provided for His people who were in slavery in Egypt.

The term "Passover" comes from the moment when Hebrew families shed the blood of a spotless lamb and sprinkled it over their doorpost so the angel of death would pass over their homes and spare their firstborn sons.

The angel did not spare the firstborn sons of Egypt, even in the palace. This plague caused Pharoah to finally relent. He told Moses to go and take the people of Israel with him. This sounds barbaric, until you remember the story of the Exodus begins with Pharoah killing every Hebrew baby because they had grown too numerous and he wanted to strengthen his control over his slaves.

As you consider this story you may wonder, *What kind of story is this? What kind of God would allow this to happen?* These questions are worth asking and they bring us back to where we started.

On His last night with His friends, Jesus forever changed the Passover. The old covenant happened in Egypt with the blood of a lamb. Jesus tells them, "Tonight I bring a new covenant—not from an animal, but from my blood."

Because of His great love, God the Father is bringing to an end the old system of sacrifices, tabernacles, and altars. Once and for all, the debt of sin will be paid through the perfect, one-time sacrifice of the spotless, blameless lamb of God.

The Son of Heaven will shed His blood and place it on the doorpost of the universe so every person, from every nation, can be included in the family of God.

NOTES

ONCE AND FOR ALL, THE DEBT OF SIN WILL BE PAID THROUGH THE PERFECT, ONE-TIME SACRIFICE OF THE SPOTLESS, BLAMELESS LAMB OF GOD.

Passage

1 CORINTHIANS 11:23-26

23 For I received from the Lord what I also passed on to you: The Lord Jesus, on the night he was betrayed, took bread, 24 and when he had given thanks, he broke it and said, "This is my body, which is for you; do this in remembrance of me." 25 In the same way, after supper he took the cup, saying, "This cup is the new covenant in my blood; do this, whenever you drink it, in remembrance of me." 26 For whenever you eat this bread and drink this cup, you proclaim the Lord's death until he comes.

HEBREWS 9:15

For this reason Christ is the mediator of a new covenant, that those who are called may receive the promised eternal inheritance—now that he has died as a ransom to set them free from the sins committed under the first covenant.

NOTES

HEBREWS 9:19-22

19 When Moses had proclaimed every command of the law to all the people, he took the blood of calves, together with water, scarlet wool and branches of hyssop, and sprinkled the scroll and all the people. 20 He said, "This is the blood of the covenant, which God has commanded you to keep." 21 In the same way, he sprinkled with the blood both the tabernacle and everything used in its ceremonies. 22 In fact, the law requires that nearly everything be cleansed with blood, and without the shedding of blood there is no forgiveness.

HEBREWS 10:10

And by that will, we have been made holy through the sacrifice of the body of Jesus Christ once for all.

NOTES

What Does This Mean for Us?

NOTES

LUKE 22:19-20

¹⁹ And he took bread, gave thanks and broke it, and gave it to them, saying, "This is my body given for you; do this in remembrance of me."

²⁰ In the same way, after the supper he took the cup, saying, "This cup is the new covenant in my blood, which is poured out for you."

You may recognize Paul's words in 1 Corinthians 11 as one of the traditional passages that accompany the celebration of Communion. This is because the sacrament of Communion is an intentional affirmation of the covenant promise of God that followers of Jesus have celebrated from the very beginning.

This is why Paul starts by saying, "I got this from the Lord and I'm passing it on to you." The early believers got it from the disciples who received it from the Lord. He told them to do it in remembrance of Him.

As we have seen, this new covenant is only possible because of the blood of Jesus. We drink grape juice to remember and celebrate the blood.

It's why we sing about the blood. It's why we say there is power in the blood. It's why we say the blood of Jesus saves us.

In the old covenant, without the shedding of blood, without the sacrifice, the sin was not forgiven. The high priest was the only one who went into the Holy of

Holies to offer sacrifices on behalf of the people on one special day of the year. The presence of God was so strong it would kill anyone who violated God's detailed instructions, because sin can't survive in the presence of a Holy God.

The veil (curtain) separating God's presence from the people was three or four inches thick. When Jesus dies on the cross and utters the phrase "It is finished," He is referring to both the sacrificial system and the veil separating God's presence from mankind. This is why the writers of the Gospels tell us the curtain tore in that moment.

Because of the sacrifice of Jesus there is no longer a separation between the people and the presence of God.

This is why Hebrews 9 and 10 summarize and contrast the details of the old covenant with what Jesus accomplished. It took time for early Jewish followers of Christ to understand that the old covenant had been completed.

The disciples knew because Jesus had made it clear to them.

Jesus did not tell us to proclaim His death because He wants us to feel sorry for Him and what He suffered. This proclamation reminds us where we stand with God.

In 2 Corinthians 5:21 Paul tells us, "God made Him who had no sin to be sin for us so that in Him we might become the righteousness of God."

By this point you see the covenant language. The "Him" in the verse is Jesus. God assumes the responsibility to make the partnership right. Remember, "righteousness of God" is a term that describes a legal standing pronounced over someone like a verdict.

NOTES

MATTHEW 27:51
At that moment the curtain of the temple was torn in two from top to bottom. The earth shook, the rocks split.

MARK 15:38
The curtain of the temple was torn in two from top to bottom.

LUKE 23:45
. . . for the sun stopped shining. And the curtain of the temple was torn in two.

NOTES

As elaborate as the old sacrifices were, they are no longer necessary. Some of us prefer great personal sacrifice because it makes us feel like somehow we've earned God's forgiveness.

But this is not what God asks for. It either wears us out or fills us with pride. We can't meet the conditions of a perfect God. We need a perfect substitute to give us His perfect righteousness.

This is who Jesus is. This is what He has done. This is why we have confidence where we stand with God.

Have you tried to sacrifice to earn God's love and approval? How did it make you feel? How did it make you feel about other people?

Do you have confidence where you stand in your relationship with this perfect God? Remember how intricate, how serious, and how deadly the old covenant sacrifices were to the people of God? Do you have a healthy respect for the holiness of God's presence?

And yet Jesus is the guarantee of a better covenant. A once-and-for-all sacrifice.

Our confidence in our relationship with God does not come from what we have done but from what Jesus has done for us.

What Do I Do with This?

SUMMARY

We cannot earn God's love and approval. We are not entitled to His promises. But we can be confident in them because of what Jesus has done for us.

As a result, Jesus has become the guarantee
of a better covenant.

Hebrews 7:22 (CEB)

QUESTIONS

01   What was your greatest takeaway from this chapter?

02   Hebrews 7:22 tells us that Jesus is the guarantee of a new and better covenant. What does the word "guarantee" mean? How does that apply to God's covenant with us?

03   **Read 2 Corinthians 5:21.** According to this verse, what did God do to Jesus, and what does He do for us?

04   Why did we need a substitute for our sin?

05   Have you ever tried to earn God's love or approval?
What was that like?

06   What's the difference between earning God's love and receiving His love?
Which do you gravitate more toward—earning or receiving?

07   How confident do you feel in your relationship with God?
What is your confidence based on?

08   After reading this chapter, do you have a greater appreciation
for the magnitude of what Jesus did for us? Explain.

WEEK
THREE

WHAT DOES GOD PROMISE
FOR MY GUILT & FAILURE?

Concept

It can happen so easily:

- Because you're busy, stressed, and out of your normal routine, you end up eating what's fast, convenient, and fried. You know your body will regret it.
- You agree to something at work you can't actually deliver, so you violate your integrity to get the project finished.
- Your lack of emotional energy and your frustration cause you to snap at your kids and say something more hurtful than you thought possible.
- You knew your relationship with your spouse was drifting, but you had no idea they were so unhappy they were preparing to leave.

If any of these situations sounds even vaguely familiar, you know what happens next. You feel guilty. You beat yourself up. You agonize over what you could have done differently. You scold yourself for lacking the self-control to avoid this mess.

The shame of what others will think and the lies of the enemy make you want to isolate yourself. *You* don't even want to be around you.

We all know how damaging guilt and failure can be. And we know they never lift us up—they only drive us deeper in discouragement.

What can we do about it?

NOTES

Most of us try to perform our way out of our guilt. We believe if we can right these wrongs through outstanding achievements, we can overshadow the haunting feeling of not measuring up.

Life becomes an exercise in reputation management. This often works really well for a while, but before long, it becomes exhausting.

Even when we succeed, we end up on a performance treadmill. The moment we step off, our cover will be blown and people will see our failures. This approach is exhausting.

There has to be a better way.

NOTES

Context

Jesus is early in His ministry. Recently He called two sets of brothers who were fishermen to drop their nets and follow Him. They responded not because it was a good career move but because they had never seen anyone like Him.

Jesus had been preaching and healing the sick, and people were coming from all over just to get close to Him. One day while He's teaching a group of religious leaders and crowds of people who traveled over a week to see Him, a group of people carried their paralyzed friend on a stretcher. When they couldn't get near Jesus, instead of giving up, they climbed up on the roof and lowered their friend right next to Him.

The Bible does not tell us how this man ended up paralyzed, but we do know, in their culture, the assumption would have been his sickness was the result of the judgment of God. Their thinking was that the fact he was crippled was not an accident—it was punishment. His paralysis was the evidence of his (or his family's) guilt.

Passage

LUKE 5:20-26

20 When Jesus saw their faith, he said, "Friend, your sins are forgiven."

21 The Pharisees and the teachers of the law began thinking to themselves, "Who is this fellow who speaks blasphemy? Who can forgive sins but God alone?"

22 Jesus knew what they were thinking and asked, "Why are you thinking these things in your hearts? 23 Which is easier: to say, 'Your sins are forgiven,' or to say, 'Get up and walk'? 24 But I want you to know that the Son of Man has authority on earth to forgive sins." So he said to the paralyzed man, "I tell you, get up, take your mat and go home." 25 Immediately he stood up in front of them, took what he had been lying on and went home praising God. 26 Everyone was amazed and gave praise to God. They were filled with awe and said, "We have seen remarkable things today."

NOTES

What Does This Mean for Us?

NOTES

We feel guilty because we are guilty. Every one of us has blown it. No one had to teach us to be selfish, to hurt others with our words, or to follow our desires no matter how it impacted anyone else.

This is why we feel guilty. The question is, what do we do with our guilt?

LUKE 5:24
"But I want you to know that the Son of Man has authority on earth to forgive sins."

It may not be obvious to us, but in Luke 5:24, Jesus is making the point that it is easier to heal a paralyzed person than to forgive their sins. We think, *What's the big deal? Just tell him he's forgiven.*

Maybe the more important question is, which is the bigger problem? Most of us would say being paralyzed because it completely changes your everyday life. In the ancient world, they understood being guilty of sin changes your eternity—both in this life and in the life to come.

The Pharisees knew no matter who you were, even if you could heal someone and help them get up off the mat, you could not forgive their sin. Because every sin is an offense, a betrayal, a rebellion against God; only God can forgive sin.

In the interim, under the old covenant, only the high priest could temporarily forgive sin on the day of atonement.

Jesus skips the whole sacrificial atonement process and tells the man his sins are forgiven.

We see this pattern repeatedly. In John chapter 8 Jesus comes into the temple courts at dawn and the Pharisees bring in a woman they've caught committing adultery. Their goal is to trap Jesus in a moral dilemma and force Him to stone the woman in accordance with their application of the law of Moses.

Imagine being this woman. This would have been an incredibly traumatic way to start the day. You'd never forget a moment like this. You'd carry the shame of it for the rest of your life.

But Jesus bends down and writes something in the dirt. We do not know what He wrote, but it drove away the majority of the crowd—especially the most vocal accusers. He tells the crowd that the first person to throw a rock at the woman should be someone who perfectly kept the law of Moses.

He asks the woman, "Has no one condemned you?" She says, "No one." He then tells her He doesn't condemn her and to go and sin no more.

In John 12:47 Jesus declares He did not come to judge the world but to save it. Hebrews 10:19-23 explains we have confidence to enter the Holy Place only because of the perfect blood of Jesus that was shed on our behalf. We can draw near to God without a guilty conscience— not because we are perfect, but because of Jesus' perfect obedience He gives to us.

NOTES

JOHN 12:47
"If anyone hears my words but does not keep them, I do not judge that person. For I did not come to judge the world, but to save the world."

HEBREWS 10:19-23
[19] Therefore, brothers and sisters, since we have confidence to enter the Most Holy Place by the blood of Jesus, [20] by a new and living way opened for us through the curtain, that is, his body, [21] and since we have a great priest over the house of God, [22] let us draw near to God with a sincere heart and with the full assurance that faith brings, having our hearts sprinkled to cleanse us from a guilty conscience and having our bodies washed with pure water. [23] Let us hold unswervingly to the hope we profess, for he who promised is faithful.

NOTES

We cannot perform our way out of our guilt. The only way out is to exchange our guilt for Jesus' perfect obedience. This is the message of the gospel.

To be condemned is to be found guilty. But for those who are in Christ, there is no longer any condemnation, because when God looks at us, He does not see our failure but the perfect righteous record of His Son.

When we feel guilty, when we feel ashamed, when the enemy accuses us, we don't jump back on the performance treadmill. We remind ourselves who we belong to.

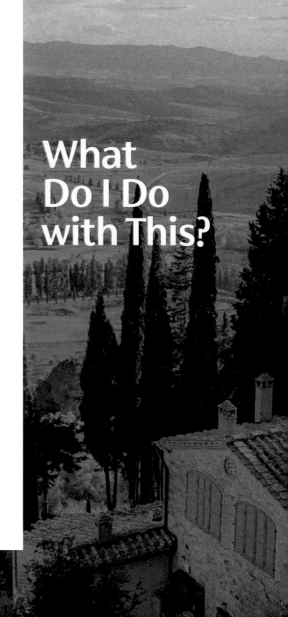

What Do I Do with This?

What do you do when you feel guilty?

Do you deny your guilt and pretend like nothing happened?

Do you put on a brave face and act like everything's okay?

Do you look for something or someone to blame?

Do you try to make up for your guilt by doing good things?

None of these options has the power to make you whole. At best, they are temporary solutions.

The only lasting, effective way to overcome your guilt is to exchange your mistakes for the perfect obedience of Jesus and find your identity and peace in Him.

SUMMARY

God's answer for our guilt and failure is not "work harder." Instead, we exchange our guilt for Jesus' perfect obedience.

So now there is no condemnation for those
who belong to Christ Jesus.

Romans 8:1 (NLT)

QUESTIONS

01 **Read Romans 8:1.** What does it mean to have "no condemnation" when you are in Christ Jesus?

02 Have you ever felt caught on the performance treadmill? Tell us about it.

03 Why is the performance treadmill so dangerous?

04 Whenever you feel guilty, which response do you typically gravitate to:
- Deny your guilt and pretend like nothing happened?
- Put on a brave face and act like everything is fine?
- Blame someone or something else?
- Try to make up for it by doing good things?

05   What is the right way to respond when we feel guilty? What should we do?

06   How does God respond to our sin and guilt?

07   Tell us about a time you struggled with guilt and experienced God's forgiveness and grace.

08   Are you struggling with guilt over something in your life right now? If so, why, and what would God say to you?

WEEK FOUR

WHAT ARE GOD'S PROMISES
FOR MY FAMILY, MY MARRIAGE,
& MY CHILDREN?

Concept

If there is one area where we want to know God's covenant promises for our lives, it's our family. Our marriage. Our children.

The health of these relationships determines the quality of our lives. We know God was right when He said it is not good for us to be alone. God is a relational God—and we've been made in His image.

If you are a parent, you know you can only be as happy as your unhappiest child. There is no pain like kid pain.

So when our kids are in pain, our marriage is struggling, or we are in constant family drama with siblings or in-laws, what we really want to know is, "Can I count on God's promises for my family?"

From the beginning of God's Word to the end, we see the answer to the question. There is no family in the Bible that escapes challenges and difficulty. But every family in the Bible has the opportunity to experience God's blessing when they commit to God's pattern.

The key issue is that there are so many voices in culture that want to shape and define what it means to be a family. We are free to choose whatever definition we like. But we also must remember: Whoever we trust to define our family is also who we look to in order to provide for our family.

God does not force His standards on us. Instead, He invites us into the covenant promises He provides when we embrace His patten for our homes.

EVERY FAMILY IN THE BIBLE HAS THE OPPORTUNITY TO EXPERIENCE GOD'S BLESSING WHEN THEY COMMIT TO GOD'S PATTERN.

NOTES

Context

In our modern world, the marriage relationship is the clearest example of the concept of covenant. A man and his family join a woman and her family in a partnership for a new family. This is no small moment—it comes with great celebration under the covering and authority of God.

GENESIS 1:27-28a

27 So God created mankind in his own image, in the image of God he created them; male and female he created them.

28 God blessed them and said to them, "Be fruitful and increase in number; fill the earth and subdue it."

You do not wear your normal everyday clothes to this moment. The vows and the rings are symbolic of the intention of a lasting covenant partnership. The message points us back to the One who created this moment and what He had in mind when He gave us this picture.

There are many parallels between weddings and our relationship with God:

- Jesus' first miracle takes place at a wedding.
- Jesus compared our perfect lives in eternity to a marriage celebration.
- Jesus used the image of inviting guests to a wedding, to God inviting people into a relationship with Him.

In Genesis 1, God makes mankind in His image—male and female—places them in His garden, and tells them to be fruitful and multiply and take care of everything He has given them.

In Genesis 2, the Bible gives more detail to this covenant agreement. Because it was not good for him to be alone and there was no helper suitable for Adam, God makes Eve. God tells Adam that Eve is bone of his bones and flesh of his flesh—they were created to be one. And they were naked and felt no shame.

This is the pattern. It does not change. Thousands of years later, Jesus reminds the people of this unchanging pattern. And in Paul's letter to the Ephesians, under the inspiration of the Holy Spirit, he affirms this covenant and explains it is the best way to understand how Jesus loves and serves His Church.

The groom loves and serves the bride not out of what she does for him but because of his commitment to God. The same is true for the bride—she honors and respects her husband out of her love for God.

The family is God's idea. It is how He builds. So when we commit to do this according to His pattern, He promises to give us His power.

Because families are made up of imperfect people, misunderstandings, unmet expectations, hurt feelings, and selfish choices will happen. But because of the covenant promises of God, forgiveness, restoration, and peace are possible.

In Matthew chapter 19, Jesus is teaching huge crowds in Galilee and the Pharisees come to Jesus and try to trick Him based on marriage technicalities in the law given to Moses.

He brings them back to the larger purpose of family.

NOTES

GENESIS 2:20b-25

[20b] But for Adam no suitable helper was found. [21] So the Lord God caused the man to fall into a deep sleep; and while he was sleeping, he took one of the man's ribs and then closed up the place with flesh. [22] Then the Lord God made a woman from the rib he had taken out of the man, and he brought her to the man.

[23] The man said, "This is now bone of my bones and flesh of my flesh; she shall be called 'woman,' for she was taken out of man."

[24] That is why a man leaves his father and mother and is united to his wife, and they become one flesh.

[25] Adam and his wife were both naked, and they felt no shame.

NOTES

Passage

MATTHEW 19:3-6

3 Some Pharisees came to him to test him. They asked, "Is it lawful for a man to divorce his wife for any and every reason?"

4 "Haven't you read," he replied, "that at the beginning the Creator 'made them male and female,' 5 and said, 'For this reason a man will leave his father and mother and be united to his wife, and the two will become one flesh'? 6 So they are no longer two, but one flesh. Therefore what God has joined together, let no one separate."

What Does This Mean for Us?

NOTES

Family is not structured like a technical contract where you search the fine print to see what you can get away with. This is the assumption of culture: The purpose of family is to make us happy. Even with the best of intentions, this strategy doesn't work. This is how families are separated—each member decides to pursue their own interests at the expense of others.

The Bible makes it clear the family is joined together by God. He blesses our families as we see them the way He sees them.

We love and serve each other out of our love for Him. This does not mean we can control or manipulate each other's actions. Every person has to choose to obey, choose to forgive, and choose to honor their commitment to God in the way they love their family.

Sometimes people do not honor these choices. Sometimes this covenant agreement is broken. In Matthew 19:9 Jesus says divorce is allowed when one of the members commits adultery. In Malachi 2:16 God says, "I hate divorce..." because He knows the impact it has on the family (NASB).

He loves the people, but He hates what the breaking of a covenant does to a family. His desire is not to judge and condemn, but to redeem and restore the lives of those who are ready and willing to receive Him.

We cannot control our family, but no one has more influence—for good or for bad—than your family.

It is not loving to constantly remind each other of past mistakes. Our families experience the love and peace of God when we love each other the way He loves us— merciful and compassionate, slow to anger, quick to forgive, abounding in faithfulness.

When husbands love and serve their wives out of their obedience to Christ, the home is blessed. When wives love and respect their husbands out of their gratitude to Jesus, the home is blessed. When children honor their father and mother, the home is blessed.

This may sound crazy. It may seem impossible. Even the best families cannot find the motivation to live this way from shared interests/personalities, amazing traditions, or the most life-changing family vacation.

In each of these situations, the family member is making a choice to honor the covenant promise of God in their heart and can expect God to bless them as a result.

When each family member understands how much Jesus loves and forgives them, they're empowered to love and forgive each other. This is the only motivation that lasts.

You may say, "My family is different. I've tried to love them and they always let me down." There is not a single family in the Bible without challenges. It is not a book filled with perfect people who can't relate to our pain.

Do not waste your emotional energy on what everyone

NOTES

EXODUS 34:6b (NASB)
The Lord, the Lord God, compassionate and merciful, slow to anger, and abounding in faithfulness and truth.

EPHESIANS 6:1-3
[1] Children, obey your parents in the Lord, for this is right. [2] "Honor your father and mother"—which is the first commandment with a promise— [3] "so that it may go well with you and that you may enjoy long life on the earth."

NOTES

else does or does not do. Instead, commit to love and serve your family the best way you can based on how Jesus has loved you.

Our motivation to love and forgive our family does not come from willpower or their performance. It only comes from Jesus. Ephesians 4:32 tells us, "Be kind and compassionate to one another, forgiving each other, just as in Christ God forgave you."

When we live this way, we can count on God's faithfulness to His promise to bless our family—even when it does not feel like it.

What Do I Do with This?

We all slip into focusing on what our family is or is not doing for us. Instead, focus on what you can do for your family.

01 Commit to pray for at least one member of your family every day for the next week.

02 Write an encouraging text or note to three different members of your family this week.

03 Pick a night at dinner this week and take a moment for each family member to say one thing about their family they're grateful to God for.

SUMMARY

The family is God's idea. It is how He builds. When we commit our family to His pattern, He promises to give us His power.

Be kind and compassionate to one another, forgiving each other, just as in Christ God forgave you.

Ephesians 4:32

QUESTIONS

01   **Read Matthew 19:4-6.** What do you think it means to become "one flesh" with your spouse? How does this affect how a husband and wife should treat each other?

02   The assumption of culture is that family is supposed to make us happy. Why does that strategy fail?

03   What is God's plan for the family?

04   Families only work when we love and serve each other out of a love for God. Do you agree or disagree? Explain.

05 What are some of the greatest challenges you've faced in your family in the past? How could this chapter apply to those challenges?

06 Are you facing any challenges in your family right now? What are they, and what could God be doing in those situations right now?

07 What is something you will do to love and serve your family this week?

● **Let's get practical: Spend a minute to pray and ask God to bring specific family members to your mind. Write down their names and what you will do to serve them and show them love. If you feel comfortable, share this list with your Small Group and ask them to pray for you this week as you serve your family.**

WEEK FIVE

WHAT DOES GOD PROMISE
FOR MY LONELINESS?

NOTES

Concept

*No society has ever had more
access to information than ours.*

*Never before has the average person been
able to instantly communicate via video to friends
and loved ones around the world.*

*Never before have we been more aware
of what the people in our lives are doing on a
moment-by-moment basis.*

And yet, never before has the Surgeon General of the United States declared a "loneliness epidemic." This changed in 2017.

Research shows loneliness is more than a negative emotion that promotes anxiety and depression. Extended loneliness is as hard on your heart as obesity or chronic cigarette smoking.

*In a recent study, 1 in 6 people (16 percent) said
they're lonely all the time. 33 percent said they felt lonely
at least once per day. More than 50 percent said
they feel lonely at least once a week.*

These numbers may be even larger because many people are embarrassed to admit they're lonely. Lonely doesn't mean alone—one of the most common modern forms of loneliness is "crowded loneliness."

NOTES

This phrase describes the experience of being surrounded by people while feeling overlooked, unseen, misunderstood, and without meaningful connection.

One of the reasons to describe loneliness as an epidemic is because it's contagious; it spreads from person to person. You are 52 percent more likely to feel lonely if you are around another lonely person.

Another surprising finding is that loneliness impacts young people more than older people. The average 60-year-old reports a higher level of joy and fulfillment than the average 20-year-old.

Loneliness is highest for people in significant life transition—going to college, taking a new job, the first year of marriage, because we expect these changes to add to our current level of fulfillment instead of transforming our relationships and support system.

God understands how significant this challenge is to our overall well-being. The Bible is filled with stories of people who experienced deep loneliness and isolation.

But in every situation, God promised to set the lonely in loving, life-giving relationships. These same covenant promises are available to us.

NOTES

Context

In the book of Ruth, during a terrible famine, Naomi loses her sons and her husband. She tells her daughters-in-law to abandon her, save themselves, and return to their homeland in the hopes they might survive.

David spent so many days alone in the pasture, his own father forgot about him on the biggest day in the history of the family—when the prophet came looking for the next king.

This was a constant struggle for David throughout his life. He was constantly on the run and afraid for his life. He regularly felt like everyone was against him and no one understood what he was going through.

In Psalm 25:16 David prays from a place of deep emotional anguish:

> *Turn to me and be gracious to me,*
> *for I am lonely and afflicted.*

In 1 Kings 19, after God miraculously moved through Elijah and defeated the prophets of Baal, Elijah ran and hid in a cave. When God asks him what's wrong, Elijah tells God he's all alone. He's the only one who obeys God and now everyone wants to kill him. God patiently reminds Elijah there are thousands of people who love God.

When Jesus starts His ministry in Luke 4, He's led out into the wilderness alone to be tempted by Satan. Luke 5:16 tells us Jesus repeated this pattern and would withdraw to lonely places to pray.

But on the night Jesus was betrayed, when He was preparing for the cross by praying in the Garden of Gethsemane, He asked His three closest friends to pray and support Him. Three times they failed Him and fell asleep (see Matthew 26:36-46).

Earlier that same night, Jesus gives us a window into a covenant promise of God that goes all the way back to the first Garden (Eden). He does not promise we won't be lonely, but He does show us God's solution to loneliness.

NOTES

LUKE 4: 1-2a
[1] Jesus, full of the Holy Spirit, left the Jordan and was led by the Spirit into the wilderness, [2] where for forty days he was tempted by the devil.

LUKE 5:16
But Jesus often withdrew to lonely places and prayed.

Passage

JOHN 15:12-17

12 My command is this: Love each other as I have loved you. 13 Greater love has no one than this: to lay down one's life for one's friends. 14 You are my friends if you do what I command. 15 I no longer call you servants, because a servant does not know his master's business. Instead, I have called you friends, for everything that I learned from my Father I have made known to you. 16 You did not choose me, but I chose you and appointed you so that you might go and bear fruit—fruit that will last—and so that whatever you ask in my name the Father will give you. 17 This is my command: Love each other.

NOTES

What Does This Mean for Us?

NOTES

Remember, this is the same night and the same conversation when Jesus said His new covenant had come through His blood to fulfill and expand the old covenants. It is a better covenant.

This is all covenant language: Love as I have loved you. Lay down your life for your friends. Everything I have learned I have made known to you. You did not choose me but I chose you to go and bear fruit. Whatever you ask in my name will be given to you.

This is how partners joined together in purpose talk to each other. These are promises that create supernatural connection.

And this is how God deals with our loneliness. The cure for loneliness is intimacy. Intimacy is the result of shared purpose.

This is why research shows friends often have more power to overcome loneliness than family, because you're born into a family, but you intentionally choose and build friendships.

PSALM 68:6a
God sets the lonely in families...

God sets the lonely in families (see Psalm 68:6a)—we call this "spiritual family." The same God who loves you so much that He sent His Son to die in your place so you could have a genuine relationship with Him, has people He places you with.

And those people have a purpose. This is God's Church—His family on the earth committed to His purpose. Ephesians 4:16 tells us the church grows and builds itself up in love as each part does its work.

When you offer your gifts to serve others out of your love for Jesus with the people He's placed you with, you find a fulfillment loneliness can't take away.

In 1 Corinthians 12, Paul describes how the different people, the different parts of a church work together toward the common good. Verse 18 says God places every part, every person in the church, just where He wants them.

There is no perfect church, but God places every person in relationship with Him in the perfect spot for them.

But God does not stop there—He calls us His friends.

This does not mean we won't feel lonely but it does give us the blueprint for overcoming loneliness. Jesus does not start by saying "make sure everyone else takes the time to understand and hear you." He says "love others the way I have loved you. Lay down your life."

All of the research points to the same solution: When we're lonely, what we need are healthy relationships. It sounds counterintuitive, but we cannot have healthy relationships when we start from what other people can do for us. Transactional relationships do not produce genuine intimacy.

This only comes when we start by loving others the way Jesus loves us and laying down our lives for someone else.

NOTES

EPHESIANS 4:16
From him the whole body, joined and held together by every supporting ligament, grows and builds itself up in love, as each part does its work.

1 CORINTHIANS 12:18
But in fact God has placed the parts in the body, every one of them, just as he wanted them to be.

What Do I Do with This?

Have you ever heard of the concept of "spiritual family"?

Do you know where God has placed you?

What does it mean for Jesus to call us His friends?

Based on how Jesus describes this relationship, how does it change the way you treat the people in your life?

SUMMARY

God does not promise we won't be lonely—but He does promise a solution. He places us in His family and gives us His purpose.

God sets the lonely in families...

Psalm 68:6a

QUESTIONS

01 What do you think it means when the Bible says, "God sets the lonely in families" (Psalm 68:6)?

02 Read the statistics about loneliness again on page 109. Why do you think loneliness is at an all-time high in our culture today?

03 **Read John 15:12-13.** What is the Bible's solution for loneliness?

04 Our culture would say that the cure for loneliness is being understood and heard. How is the Bible's message about loneliness different from culture's message?

05 What do you think it means to be part of a spiritual family?

06 Have you ever experienced spiritual family in your life? Explain.

07 Do you ever struggle with loneliness? Why or why not?

08 What do you think this statement means: Intimacy is a result of shared purpose? Do you agree with the statement? Explain.

09 What is something you can do this week to reach out to others and show them love?

WEEK
SIX

WHAT DOES GOD PROMISE FOR
MY PAIN & MY CHALLENGES?

NOTES

Concept

Our ability to trust in a promise is greatly influenced by our circumstances. There is no doubt it is easier to have hope for tomorrow when things are good today.

Pain puts our confidence to the test. When we are suffering, when we feel like we are being punished for poor choices, it becomes very difficult to lean on God's Word.

Forget a guarantee; we wonder if we even have a chance.

This is why God swore on His own name—not for the easy days, but for the impossible ones.

We have learned how this incredibly bold claim in Hebrews 6 produces encouragement and an anchor for our soul. When Paul talks about this same covenant God made with Abraham, the Bible says in Romans 4:18, "Against all hope, Abraham in hope believed..." Some versions say, "In hope against hope..."

When we are in pain, it feels like something is hoping against us. If the pain is strong enough, it feels like the whole world is against us. This kind of pain transforms us.

This struggle is common throughout the Bible but maybe nowhere more than the psalms. There is a whole category of these sad songs that detail suffering and agonizing pain—they're called "psalms of lament." The lament psalms are the most common type of song and they make up 40 percent of Psalms.

PAIN PUTS OUR CONFIDENCE TO THE TEST.

NOTES

MATTHEW 27:46
About three in the afternoon Jesus cried out in a loud voice, "Eli, Eli, lema sabachthani?" (which means "My God, my God, why have you forsaken me?").

PSALM 22:1
My God, my God, why have you forsaken me? Why are you so far from saving me, so far from my cries of anguish?

PSALM 22:24
For he has not despised or scorned the suffering of the afflicted one; he has not hidden his face from him but has listened to his cry for help.

Remember, this was ancient Israel's worship book. When we understand how many of their worship songs come from a place of pain, it helps us learn how to process our pain today.

The most famous psalm of lament is Psalm 22. It painstakingly details the impact of all kinds of torment.

It starts with the simple phrase "My God, my God, why have you forsaken me?" Jesus quotes these words from the cross.

But neither the psalm nor the story of Jesus end at this point of desperation. Verse 24 reminds us that God does not scorn or despise those in pain. He does not hide His face or ignore their cries.

In the moments leading up to Jesus' greatest suffering—including the most humiliating and painful death imaginable—He continues to trust and lean on the promises of God. His confidence in God was so great, Jesus believed not even death itself could separate Him from the love and goodness of God.

And in doing so, He makes it possible for us to do the same.

NOTES

Context

Once again, we return to the night when Jesus forever changed the way we relate to the promises of God. This is the same night as the Last Supper that we looked at in 1 Corinthians 11.

Jesus intentionally uses profoundly covenantal language to communicate His point to His followers.

He wants them to understand that when He makes a promise, it is more than the encouraging words of a friend.

Because of His relationship with God, because He and the Father are One, whenever Jesus speaks, He carries the same authority, the same guarantee, and the same eternal, life-giving words of the Father.

This is more than one of the richest theological passages in the Bible. This happened to real people, at a real place, in real time.

Imagine how you would have felt if you had been there.

The greatest person they had ever known, the great teacher, the miracle worker, the one they left everything to follow, the friend who sticks closer than a brother,

NOTES

would be violently and unjustly betrayed and arrested right in front of them.

He would be taken to the home of the high priest—someone who claimed to speak for God but wanted nothing more than to kill Jesus. He had a prison cell beneath his house. The next day Jesus would be beaten beyond the point of recognition, stripped naked, paraded through the city, and executed publicly in a manner so vicious that it could not be done to a Roman citizen.

The clear message being communicated was: If you're with Him, we'll do the same to you.

This is more than the traumatic pain of seeing the person you love murdered in front of you. This is having your entire way of life destroyed.

How in the world do you recover from something like that? Forget trusting the promise; how do you get out of bed the next day?

Passage

JOHN 14:1-6

1 "Do not let your hearts be troubled. You believe in God; believe also in me. 2 My Father's house has many rooms; if that were not so, would I have told you that I am going there to prepare a place for you? 3 And if I go and prepare a place for you, I will come back and take you to be with me that you also may be where I am. 4 You know the way to the place where I am going."

5 Thomas said to him, "Lord, we don't know where you are going, so how can we know the way?"

6 Jesus answered, "I am the way and the truth and the life. No one comes to the Father except through me."

NOTES

What Does This Mean for Us?

NOTES

Jesus tells His disciples not to let their hearts be troubled, because this is what our hearts do. They drift toward pain, worry, and fear.

Notice the covenant language: *You believe in God; believe also in me.*

Jesus is making the point: *When I promise you something, it is the same as when God promises you.*

And then He clarifies what He is up to: *I'm going to my Father's house to prepare a place for you.*

This is an incredible promise. Who would not want to be invited to live with the Father and Jesus in their home?

The only thing greater is the reason: so that you can be with me.

Jesus promises we will be with Him forever.

One of the best things about the disciples is, they say what we would've said had we been there. Thomas basically says, "We don't know where that is and we don't know how to get there!"

Jesus responds with one of His most profound statements in the whole Bible: *I AM the way, the truth, and the life.*

By now I'm sure you realize this is covenantal language. He is putting the responsibility of coming through for us on Himself. Like His Father, He is saying that He is the only one who can guarantee what you're looking for.

When we're in pain, like the disciples, we want to know why it happened. We want to know what will happen next. We want to know how long it will take to resolve.

We somehow believe that if we had the answers to these questions, it would take away our pain. That's not how it works.

Pain always involves loss. The only way to overcome loss is to be connected to a source who can give us everything we need. There is only One who can do that.

More than healing for our pain, He offers us Himself— the invitation to live with Him for all eternity.

How strong is Jesus' promise to be with Him? His covenant promise is so powerful not even death can stop it.

Hebrews 13:5 reminds us of Deuteronomy 31:6: *I will never leave you or forsake you.*

Eventually, we all wrestle with the specter of life's greatest pain: death. Sometimes we wrestle with the thought of our own death and sometimes it is even more painful to think about the death of a loved one.

We do not like to think about these moments until we are in a circumstance where it is all we think about.

NOTES

NOTES

Even in this place, Jesus' promise provides peace because we have a guarantee death is not the end. It is not the end for us *or* for the ones we love who have received the promise of God through Jesus.

If death could not hold Jesus, if He had the power to overcome His horrific death on a cross *and* being buried in a tomb guarded by the most powerful military force on the planet, then we too can find hope in the face of death.

We will be with Him forever. He has promised us.

What Do I Do with This?

Pain changes us. It changes the way we see ourselves, the people in our lives, the world around us, and even God Himself.

Pain makes us feel unsafe and uncertain. Pain is not rational; it's visceral. We don't understand it; we feel it. How has your pain impacted your ability to trust God? Have you questioned, "Where was God when this happened to me?"

Jesus tells us the solution to our pain is not more information or inflicting pain on others but in the person of Jesus Himself. We process our pain in His presence.

You can bring your hurts and pains to Him and exchange them for His peace. Simply tell Him what you're feeling. Be as honest as you know how; He can take it.

Then ask Him to fill you with His peace.

SUMMARY

God did not promise us a life without pain. But even in our greatest pain, He promises to be with us and to give us His peace.

"I have told you these things, so that in me you may have peace. In this world you will have trouble. But take heart! I have overcome the world."

John 16:33

QUESTIONS

01 Why does pain put our confidence in God to the test?

02 Have you ever faced something so painful that it caused you to question God or doubt His promises? Tell us about it.

03 **Read Hebrews 13:5.** How does this verse bring us comfort, even when facing pain?

04 How has God brought you comfort when you've been hurt or felt pain in your life?

05   What are some unhealthy ways people typically deal with pain?

06   What are some healthy, biblical ways to respond to pain?

07   How do you typically respond to pain? If you could map out your process for dealing with pain, what would it look like? Include both the healthy and unhealthy aspects of your process.

08   How have you experienced the pain of death in your life? What was that like? How did God bring you comfort during that time?

Scripture Cards

These Scripture memory cards correspond to the memory verse for each week in the *Promises* study.

We encourage you to memorize these verses during each week of *Promises*. To help, punch out these cards and put them somewhere visible, like the dash of your car, the back of your phone, or your bathroom mirror.

As a result,
Jesus has become
the guarantee of
a better covenant.

HEBREWS 7:22 (CEB)

For no matter how
many promises God
has made, they are
"Yes" in Christ.

**2 CORINTHIANS
1:20a (NIV)**

Therefore, the
promise comes by faith,
so that it may be by
grace and may be
guaranteed
to all Abraham's
offspring—not only to
those who are of the
law but also to those
who have the faith of
Abraham. He is the
father of us all.

ROMANS 4:16 (NIV)

Know therefore
that the Lord your
God is God; he is
the faithful God,
keeping his covenant
of love to a thousand
generations of
those who love
him and keep his
commandments.

DEUTERONOMY 7:9 (NIV)

"I have told you
these things, so
that in me you
may have peace.
In this world you
will have trouble.
But take heart!
I have overcome
the world."

JOHN 16:33 (NIV)

God sets the lonely
in families...

PSALM 68:6a (NIV)

Be kind and
compassionate
to one another,
forgiving each other,
just as in Christ God
forgave you.

EPHESIANS 4:32 (NIV)

So now there is
no condemnation for
those who belong to
Christ Jesus.

ROMANS 8:1 (NLT)

PRØMISES
CONFIDENCE FOR TODAY, A GUARANTEE FOR TOMORROW

PRØMISES
CONFIDENCE FOR TODAY, A GUARANTEE FOR TOMORROW

PRØMISES
CONFIDENCE FOR TODAY, A GUARANTEE FOR TOMORROW

PRØMISES
CONFIDENCE FOR TODAY, A GUARANTEE FOR TOMORROW

PRØMISES
CONFIDENCE FOR TODAY, A GUARANTEE FOR TOMORROW

PRØMISES
CONFIDENCE FOR TODAY, A GUARANTEE FOR TOMORROW

PRØMISES
CONFIDENCE FOR TODAY, A GUARANTEE FOR TOMORROW

PRØMISES

FOR MORE RESOURCES VISIT US ONLINE

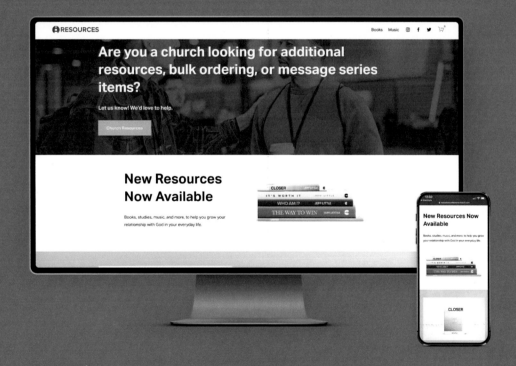

MILESTONERESOURCES.COM

RESOURCES

MILESTONERESOURCES.COM